*buckled
into the sky*

ESSENTIAL POETS SERIES 284

Guernica Editions Inc. acknowledges the support of the Canada
Council for the Arts and the Ontario Arts Council.
The Ontario Arts Council is an agency of the Government of Ontario.

We acknowledge the financial support of the Government of Canada.

buckled into the sky

Adele Graf

GUERNICA EDITIONS
TORONTO • CHICAGO • BUFFALO • LANCASTER (U.K.)
2021

Michael Mirolla, editor
David Moratto, cover and interior designer
Guernica Editions Inc.
287 Templemead Drive, Hamilton (ON), Canada L8W 2W4
2250 Military Road, Tonawanda, N.Y. 14150-6000 U.S.A.
www.guernicaeditions.com

Distributors:
Independent Publishers Group (IPG)
600 North Pulaski Road, Chicago IL 60624
University of Toronto Press Distribution (UTP)
5201 Dufferin Street, Toronto (ON), Canada M3H 5T8
Gazelle Book Services, White Cross Mills
High Town, Lancaster LA1 4XS U.K.

First edition.
Printed in Canada.

Legal Deposit—First Quarter
Library of Congress Catalog Card Number: 2020947876
Library and Archives Canada Cataloguing in Publication
Title: Buckled into the sky / Adele Graf.
Names: Graf, Adele, author.
Series: Essential poets ; 284.
Description: First edition. | Series statement:
Essential poets series ; 284 | Poems.
Identifiers: Canadiana 2020036202X |
ISBN 9781771835800 (softcover)
Classification: LCC PS8563.R3148 B83 2021 | DDC C811/.6—dc23

*always for my family
and for Ed*

*in memory of my sister Justine
1938–2015*

Contents ∼

I. He leads me in Yiddish, which I don't speak

II. "two men," I tell her one evening

III.   when the longing overtakes her

IV.   buckled into the sky

V.   early backstage

VI. Giveaway

VII. Email to Justine

VIII.   Directions to Suffern NY circa 1950

I

He leads me in Yiddish,
which I don't speak

Assupen

Born where I'm headed, my Latvian cabbie
plays disco. "Shalom Aleichem"
sways above the beat, greets me past farms
near my grandmother's home, in Assupen.
Her melody crossing the landscape
a century after she left.

The road widens and the driver gestures
at the fieldstone hospital, two hundred
years old. Next door, his mother's
cracked stucco house.

He waits for my return trip, sharing
cigarettes with men leaning against
the central barn. They smoke and banter.

I step onto unpaved paths
I'd only seen meander through
my grandmother's stories
at her long kitchen table.

I enter tall woods, white
with wild garlic. I blink
on sun-baked roads beside beet fields.
Dogs and roosters puncture the silence.

I rest under lindens that shaded
my grandmother, find doors
ajar into musty cellars.

My ears once snagged on *Assupen*'s
foreign sound. Now I hear how
my grandmother bequeathed that name.

The disco beat that skews Hebrew music
convinces me I'm on solid ground.
I could dance to its pulse, though
my feet hurt, as if I'd walked for years
toward this quiet wind
in wide plum orchards.

Armour

Because your great-grandmother Beile is long buried in Ventspils, you buttoned your all-weather tourist coat and hoped to blend into the phalanx of Latvian women. Dark hair barred you from wedging yourself among young blondes and matrons tight-lipped about old times. You had to enter dank archives to learn about your cousin Tanje and spinster aunt Pere who couldn't escape from Latvia by 1941, and your aunts Dobrah, Naftalia and Gitel, who'd also had ranks closed against them, and even Sorehenna, Rosa and Breine, whom Nazis had shot in woods near Ventspils, unshielded like your cousin Ruth (killed in knee socks). Your push to penetrate this Latvian phalanx was short-lived. You flew home and chose your own uniform. Loose jeans, with your insignia: Grossma's brooch (turquoise with silver filigree) on your T-shirt. You clasped songs of both grandmothers and six aunts, from eldest Tsvia to youngest Lieb. Safe with you here. But your insignia enlists you with all women in your tribe. Wear your uniform and feel them rustle the hairs on your skin.

inflected echoes

prayer shawls
moulder

but guttural pleas
and cadenced speech

wrap arms around my shoulders
like old Jewish uncles

and lead me back
to synagogue music

buried in grandfathers
I once knew, to news

of Latvia's
Pale of Settlement

whose Zvis and Hirsches
my open hands

unearth
and dust

She would recognize a sonnet

To collect your cash, she emerges
from her basement apartment. Into her former home,
whose high-ceilinged room you've slept in,
your clothes in her scratched armoire.
You've eaten her sausage on stained
white cloths, served by this Latvian widow
whose eyeglasses span her cheeks,
right elbow healed awry after an old break.
Now she lingers, plucking at English words
learned long ago. She talks to you of times
before "the intelligentsia" lost all they owned
down fifty years of Soviet drains.
Later, while lunch boils, she'll figure the day's receipts,
the chance to read in her chair that afternoon.

Hepatica

In Ventspils' damp
Jewish cemetery
I select
a wildflower gift
for each sister.
Three blue *hepatica*.

From soil
enriched by
our family's
bones, newborn
perennial blooms.

26 Pils Street

(in Ventspils, Latvia)

I retch, but slink inside
this apartment building's
chipped brown door.
Heave myself
up piss-stained stairs
to the second storey.

What's the story?
A chronic stomach-churner.
Here where I trespass
between spattered walls.
Where Nazis killed
my family.

Now again
boots stomp on steps below.
I stop all camera clicks
till four boys
round the landing
and mime for a photo.

One wears a red jacket.
Another grins. A tall one's arm
blocks a short one's face.
Kids, like my cousin Ruth
who'd lived in apartment 2.
Her cake, baked in 1941
left to cool.

Latvian turf

its sparse surface
a filament
that unfurls
to the land my father
lived in as a boy

this firmament
stores relics
of his first years
when Kurzeme
was Kurland

now my steps
on his soil
foment the hope
I'll find a shard
to wedge within the dust

in ferment
my mind seeks scraps
whose edge
could help me
grasp this fact—

our shared lifespan
a fragment
next to his dim time
before me, my decades
since his death

my dream that I'd spot
his hidden heart
a hundred years on
in Riga's rush-hour blare
a figment

Lion's choice

Long DNA strands: my great-grandfather's
beard. Like the wild grasses he gathers.

Nestled inside it, I ask to taste his native
field greens. The corners of his moustache rise.

Leib Wahl forages for plants in Vilnius, though
his income allows him the leisure of Torah study.

We find and savour endive, beet tops and chives.
Born before Mendel and Darwin, he hasn't heard

of mitosis or genes he might share with me:
I who lodge in his beard as my fingers

smooth tangles unseen near its centre.
Leib the Yiddish *lion*. Wahl a German *choice*.

He agrees to try my Perth greens, but his face falls
so fast I clutch hairy clumps. I braid a trail for him

in case he yearns for home. From my fridge I grab
field greens organic as his: radicchio, chicories and chard.

We devour them all, with lemon juice, garlic
and oil. He probes the plastic package.

Mouths full, we exchange names of each grass we chew.
English, German and Yiddish. *Parsley, petersilie, petrishke.*

Neither of us looks for meat or potatoes.
I dab garlic from white hairs.

after the fact
(1906–1954)

tickets and tact. tickets first for Grosspa
and Aunt Tsvia. Ventspils to New York.
tickets earned, tickets sent for Grossma
and my younger aunts. my toddler father.
new-world tact. fare barely saved for one

last ticket. earned in New York and sent
to Ventspils. for sturdy cousin Grishe,
keen to earn. save and send. Grosspa's
brothers Shollem and Levin. sisters
Breine and Pehre. Grossma's mother

Khaia. Grishe's sisters Beile and Taube.
old-world tact. Grishe ceded his ticket to
spinster Aunt Pehre. years of lace in New
York. crocheted and tatted. little earned.
nothing saved. nothing sent. Grishe at his

mother Breine's kitchen table. no tickets,
but tact. another glass of sweet tea. nine-
year view of Ventspils' harbour.
expulsion to Russia. ticket not needed.
complete lack of tact. takkety-tak-tak.

Nazi bullet attack. a truck, with Aunt
Breine pushed into its open back. her
granddaughter Ruth. Shollem. Beile.
Levin. Taube. forced dismount in woods.
tak-tak-tak. new-world pact. Aunt Pehre

taught me to knit. brought us the
samovar, buffed to a burnished brass. old-
people's tact. how do you live with these
facts. no tickets. no fare. yet you breathe
new-world air. tacit pact. airmail packets

and postcard pleas. kept between
Grosspa and Grossma. Aunt Tsvia and
Aunt Pehre. air letters folded and piled.
no rustling paper young people could
hear. new-world tact. cues copied

from elders. stuck with their lack. of
fares. of family. unable to act. closed
ticket. can't change it or go back. sisters-
in-law intact. Grossma and Aunt Pehre.
still flatmates after Grosspa's death. lived

ten years in the New York flat. L.A., five
more after that. Friday nights. a place set
for Breine or Levin? or talk just of pot
roast. can't ask. our new-world fact. we
live with our lack.

Ebreju kapi

(Latvian for *Jewish cemetery*)

Dead leaves drop
to others underfoot:
veins desiccated, leaf skin
decayed like Uncle Levin's
fingers. He beckons
me close, unfazed
that I can't read
the Hebrew names
on these headstones
razed by war.
When I step, twigs
snap like gunshot.

Moss on one grave
almost obscures
the Latin letters
that etch our name.
But I sit with Uncle Levin
anywhere here.
I don't bother with rocks
for his tombstone
to wish him eternal
life, my use for ritual
lost on this slashed
Baltic ground.

Here he lives in dark
soil splattered
by lindens and pines.
Below words or
thought, like a
grandfather's voice
or a grandson's
half-formed song.

He leads me in Yiddish, which I don't speak

This Moses dangles car keys
says *Foren*: Let's go!
and I squeeze into his Lada—

alone with this man I just met
by phone. Boxed matzo
between us, he transports me

through Ventspils. Empty
warehouses: the synagogue and yeshiva
my father's first school.

One Jewish star on the plaster wall
next to 26 Pils Street, Aunt Breine's
last address. A century peels away

like paint on the houses in this
Old Jewish Quarter. Moses buys me
maizes supe—Latvian bread pudding

warm and sweet as the life
my father passed down to me.
At a Holocaust monument

his brother carved, Moses points
to the ground. Taps his temple:
your family was smart to leave

this place where we stand together
and talk. How to tell him Aunt Breine
chose to stay. How to know

Nazis would shoot her.
Undser Yidden, he says.
Our Jews, I understand.

II

"two men," I tell her one evening

Hello and welcome to our gallery

here in Lasithi. You've come at a perfect time!
We've just updated our permanent exhibition
of windmill sculptures, on display for what
seems like two centuries. (*Pause.*) The sculptures
remain on view, as always, fading in Lasithi's
fields. But now—throughout our gallery's
lofty space, under our high azure ceiling—
you'll see we're interpreting these artworks.

Their rust and twist of metal, bleach and
crack of wood. Their towers tumbling into
wild anise. Spars that jut askew, vanes appearing
in absence. I don't need to point out (though
our signage does mention) the interplay of
texture, form and colour. Angled balance.
Flux of light, chiefly in breeze.

So, to begin! We invite you to follow our route
marked in packed dirt and Cretan stone. From
this path, you'll best observe our spare—and
random—installation, in all its diverse synthesis.

But first, a note about our prices, which do
include the sculptures' historical context. As
you may know, these windmills once watered
orange zucchini flowers and bulbous scallions.

And as you may also know, these windmills were redundant when we began to show them. So we've reduced their prices—even though, clearly, our new interpretive signs increase the sculptures' prestige!

Just a word about investment value. The worth of these avant-garde commodities will parallel—to borrow an art term—(*pause)* the rise of diagonal line. This has been reflected in a surcharge for the sculptures' accidental aesthetics.

imaginary Greek etymology

day leaks its lifeblood
smears nebulous pinks, feeble reds
across Crete's weary sky

night waits on its haunches
to consume day's remains
its tongue poised to drink this stain

till night spreads its grey coat
lopes stealthily over land
and claims its dusky prey

this ritual sundown surrender
enticed ancient Greeks to depict
twilight's open-veined pause

naming this shrouded hiatus
when airy beasts spill unearthly hues
likófos: wolf light

Milia, Crete

afterwards, he climbs the hill
with cameras and lenses
strapped to his back

below, she suns herself
on the verandah
of Cretan stone

gazes wide and high
at greens and golds
in rock outcrop

then listens while thrushes
trill round her head
sing to their mates

she sees him halfway up the slope
once more prone—
intent on mauves, blues

red and pink wildflowers
like confetti seeded
into bloom—

she shades her eyes
and rises as she watches
his tanned arms

across the gorge
up the steep, winding path—
far, even as the thrush flies

Lament on Lasithi Plateau

Alone in a Cretan field, I sigh.
White sails once billowed
across this plain. Now just my nine
dry spars clack, circling high
as the Dikti mountains around me.
I moan while wind veers my vane.
My voice screams when I'm pressed
to giddy speed. O Demeter!
I need you in my dotage.

I never craved your summertime
company. I spun on my own,
applauded your time with Persephone.
Our reunion each autumn freshened
our scheduled friendship.
A pastoral paradise, where we windmills
mingled with people and gods.

Today I watch a human below,
sinewed and stiff from years
weeding broad beans I've watered.
Like her, I lag. My pump crude,
frame rusted, though my ropes
and wires still hoist these bleached spars
and weathered sails. My shaft strains
to draw water from the aquifer.

A trickle flows into my cistern,
enough to nourish the human's
spiky artichokes, dark kale.
Seeds for next year's harvest.
Where are you, my ageless Demeter?
The earth may be your domain,
but distraught for your daughter
you've seen its underside.

Don't reveal your mysteries:
just comfort me in our longevity.
I see the John Deere engine hunkered
near potato plants, programmed
with no notion of our cultivated
history. O goddess, let that
contraption supersede me
and hasten my demise! Bid me
lay my sails on your breast.

Easy going in Greece

We're speeding down a highway
when we see a detour sign. Barricades
block the road, but you drive on.

You can't go there, I say. In high
gear, you find a gap & nudge
the roadblock with your silver car.

I'm going, you announce
as we squeeze through. The next
blockade & your same stunt

till bulldozers obstruct
our way. You don't blink.
You swerve

onto an exit that appears
just as the road ends.
My first day in this foreign land.

Weeks later, we zigzag
up a mountain road. A car at the bend
bars our route.

You gesture & shout, but at last
back up. I don't hear what
the driver mutters

though our cars inch by. You stare
ahead. Once he's past
you rev your engine, grind

gears to the top. You don't
say what you heard
in that driver's words.

Karfi

I. The last Minoans

(Minoan civilization ended on Mount Karfi, Crete, in 12th-century BC)

We can no longer smell the ocean our people sailed.
From this peak, sea merges with slate sky.

We gaze at Lasithi Plain below, the fields our ancestors farmed,
our crops left ripe when the Dorians thrust us inland

and up Mount Karfi. We marched looking back till Nissimos,
then lowered our eyes as the trail rose to our ghetto.

Hope shrivelled, though its remnant helps us survive
this arid summit. We dream of home, but for now

we've built low houses, paved roads, formed and farmed
steep terraces. At dusk, we watch bearded vultures soar

skyward, drop bones on rocks to eat the marrow.
In wind and sleet, our men stand guard against Dorians

who would slaughter us in our high jail. Our snake goddess
strengthens us to welcome births.

We sit on crags with our children, born to fettered lives,
and recall Knossos. We must return to our lands

before we all rot here in domed tombs. Yet in summer,
silent wind on our skin, the children dance

along rugged slopes. Violet flowers bloom between stones.
We eat our grain without fish.

II. The robust Dorians

(Modern Cretans descended from the Dorians)

Above Mount Karfi, vultures still skydive,
fling bones and swoop. Reject carrion

and seize what they need. Their adapted tongues
still suck marrow. And the Cretans still watch

just as the Minoans watched millennia ago
near shrines for clay gods with arms raised

to bless them. But after centuries on Karfi,
the Minoans may have lost patience with old ways.

In thirst for their green plain, perhaps
they walked down. Unless Dorians killed them,

former foes mingled. Clay gods lowered their arms
and crumbled. The Minoans' tongues

altered to speak Dorian words and taste
the zest in their neighbours' food.

sustenance

high on a three-hulled hydrofoil
skimming the Aegean from Mykonos
to Crete, she sits between her sister and
her lover in a three-seat row

a three-person sandwich: she's a
honey filling held by their bread

the lustre still thick from jam-and-butter
sandwiches she and her sister ate at school—
white bread and sugar sustaining them
through half a century, till she

and her lover cross continents
to meet her sister and feast

on crusty bread, sharp *kefalotiri*, dark
kalamata olives, orange sections centred
on her lap, as her right hand spoons quince
for her first ambrosial companion

and her left pours red wine for her lover:
well-seasoned and her last

air's drift

the long lace curtain breathes in the wind—
      puffs out, then reels in
the rosettes on its crocheted squares

while one open window, dark-framed, stays
      hinged to its hook by an iron curlicue
in this Old Jewish Quarter hotel in Rhodes

with its view of the black marble monument
      to Jews, stone cold after living here five hundred years
till July 23, 1944, when Nazis stopped their breath

sitting by the Libyan Sea

chocolate softened with Cretan sun
dissolves on my tongue

at Palékastro, where four thousand years ago
Minoans lived

grew grapes, kept bees on this
hot plain that slopes to the sea

—a Minoan cistern, a chamber
for storing grain, shards of *pithoi*

excavated in 1902, buried again
for sixty years as wind blew back the soil—

now a vinyl roof shields
dug-up graves of people

who on days like these
walked to this beach for its breeze

saw the sea's sapphire fade
as sand lapped at their feet

watched ochres separate to tans and greys
on schist islands, breathed the salt tang

that quickens rubbled facts
among low stone walls at Palékastro

from the days when Minoans squinted
in the glare and snacked

on bunches of honeyed grapes
before they returned to their town

"two men," I tell her one evening

1. two bearded men at a table
2. my table set like theirs
3. my sister next door, behind a long wall
4. an outdoor taverna in Hania, Crete

1. both men old, one looks ageless
2. rolled napkins, thick bread, bottle of Boutari
3. in words foreign to me as Greek, she prays
4. bouzouki music mournful as Jewish melody

1. they talk and gesture, slurp their wine
2. I sip: where have I seen them before?
3. she peers at Jewish stars on half-moon windows
4. *The Place*—this taverna's English name

1. the ageless one hands the other a flat stone
2. I gape: wine drips on my chin
3. my sister intones the *Sh'ma* evening prayer
4. warm olives appear near my glass

1. he calls the stone *The Ten Commandments,* calls the
   man *Moses*
2. I drain most of my wine while I gawk
3. she chants with her small congregation
4. strings of bulbs frame the cluster of tables

1. when he speaks of a covenant, light fills his face
2. I gulp what's left of my wine
3. the wall's heavy door opens
4. a fig tree flutters

1. Moses calls it a *deal*, calls him *Yahweh*
2. I watch my sister enter the taverna
3. she scans the crowd for me
4. late-day air on my arms

1. the men nod at inscriptions above the wall's door
2. I've never hankered to learn Hebrew letters
3. my sister's mouth fits Hebrew and Greek
4. several chairs scrape cement when she sits

1. their table empty as their Boutari
2. I point to their table and my own bottle
3. "Gate of the Lord," she translates. "The righteous shall enter"
4. at the place outside, they might also eat hummus

III

when the longing overtakes her

when the longing overtakes her

she sloughs off rush-hour crowds   drives
through New Brunswick's pillowed hills
cloud-daubed sky   serpentine highway
with spruce sides   sliced
granite peaks   valley sun on potato blooms
and hay   Saint John River shadowed green

tidal flats to Nova Scotia
grey whales of clouds   Canso's ocean
Cape Breton's cliffs

and she rides the ferry   ushers in
the frothed wake   balmy stern
blustery bow   first dots
of Port aux Basques   cirrus strands
over Table Mountains
and Twin Hills   *that's why*
I'm headin' home   crooned live
in the ferry lounge

she waits   for the boat's latch
onto Newfoundland   broadened roadway
near Deer Lake   sky gauze
above spruce and aspen   gusts
at Shoal Arm wharf

a small second ferry   course short
past coves   trees contoured
through fog   the car's bounce across
the timber bridge   her purple house
between the tickle and the sea

her kitchen door   propped open
to neighbours   hubbub
of terns on Lighthouse Hill
Western Cove's feathered grass   pulled tall
in wind   the Lookout's soundless waves

and in Little Bay Islands   days paced
to tides   friends known long
as family   and family
known long   as spruce   rocks
water   sky   and the wind
she first felt   as breath

They take out their albums
and out come the stories

Sue's family boat: twenty aboard
for Western Cove after Sunday dinner.
Her aunt's clapboard house on the hill.
Father pouring rum for men, women
shoeless in the sun. Purple grass billowing.
Sue and her brothers chasing cousins
who'd met them at the wharf.

Mike from away: grins on his Ski-Doo
with Liz. Owned Aunt Edna's
Boarding House just a year
before this visit. By noon
he slumped on the handlebars, heart
stopped at fifty. It took Liz two years
to drag herself back and
sell the house to Barb and Jim.

Grandma Hettie's yellow house:
blurred shots soft with fog. Jim's boyhood
naps next to Hettie's stove.
On this settee, now here
in this boarding-house kitchen
where Barb's bread smells good as Hettie's.

Uncle Ned: sat in that yellow house
for twenty-three years, legs crippled.
Cracked jokes when young Nola
stopped by with friends. Unsure whose uncle
he was, she still went round whenever she could
to pass the time, and eat
the candy he kept for them.

Ned's cousin Ray, in khaki: stands erect
for the camera the day he returned
from the war. His last picture
before he died en route to his job
at sea. His niece June says
a stray submarine killed him
in Halifax Harbour. Or he leapt from
his ship to a skiff, slipped and drowned.

Western Cove: long-stemmed grass
that weathers the seasons. I lift my Nikon
to the breeze that blows through the grass
and up around me. Onto boatloads
of airy grown-ups at Sunday supper. And
along the beach, on their full-bellied children
running in the evening light.

fog

plants a moist kiss on the mouth of the world
condenses thick breath the gods exhale at night

floats into view, melting edges as it spreads
erases footprints we tread each day

hoists its sheet above the sea
billows over cities, unites cliff and gorge

hugs us in mother's soft-fleshed arms
fluffs eiderdown for noonday naps

kneads our cares like our own masseuse
burrows in children's blanket castles

paints its lull, stretches muffled moments
deflates our focus on indexed grids

drones into our minds, sidles through dreams
swallows sunburnt history

spills its pigment onto iridescent shells
overstays its visit, steeps murky tea

blots out thoughts of polished days ahead
shading the grey passage between life and death

drowned in the Straits of Belle Isle
July 1894

a thin arched stone
aslant in
high wild roses
eye-level lupins

this trail above the cove
one strand of paths
that braid through
small graveyards—

a picket-fence plot
near the dock
and on the hill
a clan of graves

each festooned
with weatherproof tulips
then enclosed
in scalloped concrete rails

a white gravel comforter
over every coffin
so the dead stretch out
and rest among us

Jigged marbles

I

Suley Ann hanged himself, a woman says at the cove.
Why did he do it? She talks with me about this shy
Mi'kmaw who settled here and fished two hundred
years ago. Still she mourns: couldn't someone have
saved him?

II

"Aunt Bea's green house" has sold twice since
Bea moved to the mainland. As two neighbours
and I pass the house, they describe Bea's soft voice
when she came to chat, sleeves rolled high to help
knead bread.

III

Grandma Hettie's nieces and nephews sit with their
childhood friend, who offers me smoked cod. They're
on Hettie's daybed, sagged ever since her bedridden
son fed them sweets. Now grown, they recall Hettie's
sepia sisters relaxed on her flat-rock beach.

IV

Ted and Grace were ten when Grace sailed away
on the ferry. They'd grown up together inside this
town, Ted's sister explains at dinner. He gave Grace
marbles to drop in the sea, so he could always
find her again.

Lost thread

Tom Bowers fell in love with Minnie Oxford.
Without a word, he built her a house near
Suley Ann Cove. He crafted fine chairs, stocked
shelves, even threaded needles so she could sew.

Then he proposed and she refused.

Tom lived in that silent house, sewed his own
burlap clothes. He stitched a sack looped
onto a stick to bring food home. Still
he grew gaunt.

Minnie's niece pours tea in her kitchen
and tells me this tale, shows me a photo
of Tom as he strode from the store
with his stick. Everyone here, she says, knows
how his mind unravelled. Eyes feral.

One day Tom's parents walked down to his house
and found him drowned in his barrel.
Lungs full, heart collapsed.

He had turned away, frayed to the nub, but men
of the parish carried him back, buried him among
his neighbours' graves.

There he remains, Minnie's niece tells me. Part
of the fabric of this town that stretches to fit
friends of friends, near-strangers passing through

these last lived-in islands of Notre Dame Bay
before the land dips to join the sea.

IV

buckled into the sky

Onward

The sign looms midway down the hall
between Zurich's *Arrivals* and *Baggage Claim*.

Lit black background with white
Helvetica letters, printed in English.

Below, a door steers us into a chamber
whose inner gates swing open.

Each circled arrow points ahead.
A few steps before the next door opens

and we exit into a new zone, enmeshed
in crowds that stream toward more Swiss planes

to German trains en route to other places.
All with doors and gates that press us on.

A tanned family sheds Bain de Soleil's orange scent
as they hasten by. I almost slow, thoughts caught

in dusk beach light that bronzed my toddler's body
long ago, "Hey Jude" that blared between waves.

No Way Back. My pace
keeps time with fellow travellers.

Heidi costume doll talks of her sixty years as my prize in a childhood writing contest

I'm stuck in this plexiglass box. My skin has fossilized
to vinyl. At my real Heidi age, 140, whose skin stays plump?

In my prime, millions of mothers with *Heidi* daughters
    adored me.
Johanna Spyri birthed me but can't free me. She's dust.

Airborne specks obscure me. You can't see in and I can't
see out, though I'd only noticed girls who smirked

at my red dirndl, in urban rooms as small as my cage.
Frankfurt rooms like Clara's where I was trapped—

the first time I couldn't smell yellow rockroses or taste wild
strawberries. Now I can no longer bend to brooks so cold

their water bites my tongue. I'm clamped to this tin stand
between iron prongs. But if you'll let me

I'll show you fir-treed paths to sudden sunlit spaces.
Meadows still bloom behind my eyelids, even as I wither

to my caricature. My story shrivels, embodied in dolls like me
and little picture books whose covers show me nimble.

One day I saw myself in children's films on afternoon TV.
A talking dog in Swiss doll clothes moved its mouth

to my words. Another dog said Fräulein Rottenmeier's lines.
I couldn't watch, though I'd shrunk from Clara's gruff
        governess—

her skin then stiff and rouged as mine now. Below
this epidermis, I'm a mountain goat grazing on fragrant hay.

charged landscape

on the horizon
        throngs of wind turbines

       warn in semaphore
across fields and hills

    twirl as prayer wheels
    for earth's future

      above the corn
    over the land

bleached skeletons against the sky

These things happen in the news

but till now just to others. The walls of our house
barred what might strike us. Now our brothers, alone
in cars, don't return from work. None of them
call or answer their phone. Unease settles
mute among us. We report the missing: Ted
on Highway 7 from Perth, due at four. Steve
on the Queensway from Vars, expected at six.
Josh on the 40 from Hudson, at half-past five.
Inside our house, air thins till we dig deep
within ourselves to breathe. Our children lie
wide-eyed in bed. Police say our three fall
into a broad-based group. All disappeared.

Near dawn we doze in chairs, wake and call
police again for news. There is none.
Neighbours on all sides drop by, ask
about our missing, talk about their own.
We join more neighbours who've been searching
streets, stop at houses for hot soup.
                                    We find one
family's son, who'd vanished with the rest, inert
on frozen ground. The nurse from two doors down
kneels to revive him.
                        At night we see
a bus arrive, full of our lost people:
unsmiling, unharmed, weary.

On Monday Ted sets out for Perth, Steve
goes back to Vars, Josh leaves for Hudson.
By Wednesday, neighbours don't knock
on our door. They wave from cars
headed to the highway.
By the weekend, they drive past
and stare straight ahead.

afterimage

as our seaside month ebbs
we perch on this wide beach rock

watch each wave curl and stretch
hear it announce its arrival on shore

follow its furrows of undersea sand
that wobble with each undertow

then we rise, imprint our feet on dunes—
stout marks on firm sand, shallow steps

in sodden spots—and squish brief signatures
onto water's edge between erasing waves

retreat to our rock so black-backed gulls
can digest their overturned crabs

before dusk dissolves all this except
the sea's pulse, the sharp salt air

brother Karl duck?

a duck   one duck   why a duck?
swims   outside ropes   that cordon
this *Zone de Baignade   Privée*
from other water   of Lake Magog

a duck   one duck   the same duck?
swims   inside the ropes   the next day
near   where I wade
its head dipped   for bugs   it hunts
through water   clear   down to sand

a duck   illiterate   anglophone
pas un canard   social   socialist
or anarchist   swims   close to me
misses perhaps   its Marx brothers
who cavort   in their bowl   of duck soup

why a duck?   one brother   hammers
to Mr. Hammer   a hotel owner   who splutters
It's … It's deep water   this duck
either *a viaduct*   elevated   above the lake
or just   a duck   that ruffles feathers

Crescent

Waves rear and froth. They bound
like the mare onto white sand. Your scream
pierces their sudden rumble, then hovers
above the ocean.

Wind swirls the mare's mane as she sprints
unchecked down the crescent beach, whose end
fades from where I stand, my mouth
a perfect O.

That runaway mare abducts you, loud
in fright as I am mute, your father's gait
a doomed attempt to match
her headlong gallop.

Haunches drenched, at last she halts. You
slowly descend. Now decades later, what lingers
for us, below your floating shriek, is
the splendour of that beach.

Moonscape

We glance at Ming tombs, rush along
the Great Wall, crunch Beijing duck.
After our trip, we don't adjust

our watches. Home clocks set to Chinese,
we choose our night and day: thick-draped
sleep, Couche-Tard stores, unplugged phones.

Just the rare email and at hours we've reversed,
doctors' notes that postpone work. We stroll
darkened Park Street, pore through Tolstoy

and listen to whole symphonies. Or daydream
propped in bed, till this hiatus has to end.
Now we wait for another blue moon

when we'll feel grounded again. Brief
as liquid moons in Chinese myth, our own
moon time stays solid: crazy and full.

Angled

(after a watercolour by Robert Chambers, 1979)

The hut may be warmer white
than the surrounding snow
or may seem so
near winter trees
that let light fall.
It's early morning
and it's just before dusk
and it's midday shaded by cloud.
Sky has merged with ground.

Shadows tone the snow
iceberg-blue
but I'm not chilled.

Space among the trees becomes
a path to the cabin—
how long or far
hard to gauge.
Blocked, I'd thought
by a fence or gate.
Now I see it's a twig settee
angled so I can view the entrance.
A snow-soft seat.

I almost sit
but instead move forward
through shafts of light.
As I reach the door
stillness finds my skin.
I turn the knob and also
open it from within.

buckled into the sky

you pee in the sky
but when you try to sleep
in the sky

a cushion of air
yawns underneath you
into the abyss

you eat in the sky
your tray meal so small
you chew over

text on the box
of "Monty's Chicken
& Thyme Hot Wrap"

made in South Godstone UK
its palm oil more than
its 16% chicken

and while in the sky
as you stare at your screen
a cartoon paper bag

mourns its mate blown
ever closer to the vapour
of a vast paper-pulp vat

if you read in the sky
ink's straight route quivers
above the clouds

if you'd like to talk in the sky
seatmates gawk at the void
past the wing

so little chicken
confined high in air
you wait for the sky to fall

V

early backstage

Memorial to adverbs

Ellen sits alone, head bent earnestly.
Humming, she stitches the white cloth etched
in the 1826 *Illustrated English Grammar.*

> *Ellen works <u>neatly</u>, sings*
> *<u>sweetly</u>, sews <u>industriously</u>.*

She is at Starbucks. Thumbs move
fervently around her. She peeks
at two hand-held machines nearby.

> *u c girl in lng dres & hed*
> *reath like frkng Qn Vctra*
>
> *she lks crAZ sngng*
> *& sewng LOL*

Her brow smooths as raccoons
saunter across a screen, pry a bin.
She watches their busy thumbs.

"They routinely lift trash lids, invariably
strew rubbish," she remarks aloud.
Everyone dims their screen.

Hum gone, she folds her cloth, sips tea.
She looks through wide plate glass
toward the late-day sun.

A mourning dove rests
on a statue's cravat.
Ellen inhales and closes her eyes.

When she opens them, the bird has flown.
She gazes around once more as quiet people
read their machines.

"What leisure to think lucidly!" she exclaims
shutting the door firmly behind her.

a sign

TEN ANT PARKING ONLY:
spaces for ten
crummy cars
span centimetres
of a parking lot
so in proximity
black ants
can unload
morsels and tidbits
to trek
up their hill
across metres
of monotone asphalt
where soon
black rubber wheels
will roll out
ant innards
         as one day
we too will be nailed
like this sign
we scan
as we pass
too busy to pause
weighted with bags
from the deli

Economical

I

Came in cool. Am nice cool. Man, ice cool!
Anemic cool, cinema cool, iceman cool:
can ice loom?

II

Claim on eco. No Mecca oil.
Manic eco, lo!

Mail eco con! Mecca oil on, coal income.
Oil con came. No eco claim.

III

Alone comic, comical one!
A comic noel … comical eon.

IV

Coma. No lice.
Am ice colon.
Am colic one.
A colic omen: a mice colon.

V

Cocain mole. (I conceal Om.)

summed-up sonnet

it's hard to press an alphabet
of words into twelve lines
that point to one last thought
we extend to our lives

yet twelve is one half more
than western music's scale
that swells to chords
and four times more

than primary colours
that spread to blended hues—
surely then our minds will
tune and shade a lettered text

so flexed with fitting hints
we glean tomes from scant gist

Bathwater reverie

Her name is Helen.
Who Helen is you don't know
or whether she might be the baby
you shouldn't throw out when this time
in your bath is through.
Your limbs slump in womb-warm liquid.
At least you know
you must have slept, drained
of cares, stretched
in your clawfoot tub where

water oiled like the seasons
eases your slips between
drowsy sense and dreams.
When seasons slide, you lose
deep sleep. Snow loosens
to a drip, or your mind snaps open
as temperatures dip. Or autumn
oozes its doze
into pores
of your soaked sea-sponge.

And how about the framed oil painting?
Check it out as you watch weather
shift outside the window.
Or look in the gift shop
—the one you pass on your way
to the pantry, whose shelves reach
the ceiling. You must hurry
to finish the inventory.
Already Helen's framed portrait
topples from an upper shelf.

occasional poems

slouch off-duty on occasional tables
loll in occasional chairs
doze till some future noon
when they may be reborn
as free verse or with
metre or rhyme
bred from their lines

their words, wan and worn
could also slither
into oblivion
or even salmon-like
flash red skin
and spawn
just once before they die

as you, who've seized the occasion
to read so far now gauge
if this poem will sink or swim—
its red eggs crushed
under river stones
or hatched on the long route
to the sea

early backstage

clear-headed air along a canal.
octagons cracked inside its ice.
edges soft with algae.
back-door buzzer at an arts centre.
zigzagged halls in warm catacombs.
arrowed notes stuck on cinderblock.
blue *CATS* crates.
lean women buff in leotards.
feline faces greasepainted white.
tawny costumes, ruffled shoes in dressing rooms.
doors ajar, spikes of light.
soprano voice, silver from an unseen space.
rehearsal room striped in red-chair rows.
tepid plaster smell.
jangle of a coffee trolley wheeled in, then out.
silence before choir practice.
flyleaf of a music score.
feet propped on the seat ahead.
flow of my black roller pen.
glittered words:

                    fireworks while the stage is dark.

15 fragments

1

The world around me swarms with subjects:
tabby cats, fingers of snow
on spruce, Elmer Fudd, the *Goldberg
Variations*. Still my pen circles again
and again to childhood, which arcs
to fit my frame.

2

March 2015: I read a profile about
Lonni Sue Johnson in the *New Yorker*.
March 1985: I clipped the *New Yorker* cover
she drew—the only cover I've ever kept.

3

I learned that the hippocampus
encodes and connects new memories.
And after viral encephalitis
her brain can't interlock pieces
jigsawed like these stanzas.

4

The artist on her cover stands at a white
canvas in a white loft, surrounded by
large watercolours. Each
shows a sliver of buildings
seen from the loft's wide window.

5

Outside the window that spans
the cover, sunset tinges watertanks
on high-rise roofs. Its rosy wash
glows on canvasses
stacked throughout the loft.

6

Her scene is congenial. The figure
paints alone in neutral space
filled with finished pictures.

7

Colours overlap. Their tones
flow from canvasses
to the artist's clothes, blend
into views out the arched window.

8

Over thirty years, her small person
has grown into a mascot
for my verse. Now I know
she's famous for little people
like the one I seized.

9

Though she drew her artist from behind
I'm sure the unseen face is mine.

10

She lacks memories to colour
her constant present. Yet she helps me
portray my past: she drew
the tiny figure who paints
different fragments
seen through a single loft window.

11

How could I have adopted her artwork, unaware
of who she was? In all the years
she still recalled
her six *New Yorker* covers
I read nothing about her.

12

Just one more slice of her skyline, another
angle of sun. Dusk's contours
don't spark memories
for Lonni Sue Johnson, the L. S. JOHNSON
who signed her illustration.

13

As I accumulate scenes in words
my mascot cheers me on.
Contemplates a fresh canvas.
Peers once more out the window despite
piles of rose-toned paintings. Together
we gaze into waning day.

14

She remembers only the last few minutes.
Though she recognizes her style
she can't list images she once drew—
not even her painted figure
who looks out at an urban sunset.

15

Her round face rests full-page
on glossy paper. Eyes closed, half-smile
in light as soft as the scene
outside her artist's studio.

VI

Giveaway

I hear the comb caress her hair

the comb dips down and down again
to separate thick strands, her strokes slow
as she bends, movement so fluid I wonder

whether it was mother or daughter
who drove to their restaurant
and stepped behind their van
to comb her waist-length hair

black hairs spill onto black asphalt I see
through leafless trees and chain-link fence
as I stand behind glass
among barbells and treadmills

my curls sweat-soaked to my skull
while the gym clock ticks minutes
until she lifts loose oiled hair
to slant the comb through knots
close to her scalp

then sets the comb on the fender
and hand to hand ties a low ponytail
shakes the comb's stray hairs
straightens her matronly figure
and walks briskly into her kitchen

where I tell myself
she'll start to stack large jars of chutney
so I'll go back to my black iron weights
that a moment ago I could no more press

than plug headphones into the gym's TV
if I heard a diva singing melismas
under canopies of trees

Billy

First you detached his head, to hear
the hiss inside his empty skull.
Guilt's half-life lasts for decades.

You dropped his blue plaid pants,
found no boy parts traced or shaped.
Still, you'd already detached his head.

Then you dumped Billy on a shelf
but he wouldn't return to his plastic form:
his half a life in your first decade.

Time melts. Your own girls grown,
you dream a Billy who lacks any flesh.
No head you might want to detach.

He languishes on your mind's dark shelf,
marooned at its faraway end. You wince
at his half-life. Guilty for how many decades?

His were the first boy ears to hear
your thoughts, this toy you tossed in dust
soon after you unhinged his head.
Your pangs of guilt live on. Half your life.

Past the landing

Through closed eyelids
I watch Mother walk out
of my walk-in closet.

Her eyes, all sclera, observe
me in bed with Reo, tangles
of sheets around us

after love. Reo's breaths deep
and even. He doesn't see her.
Both our heads grey on the pillow.

Mother's hair a black bun
at her neck, where a sun hat
dangles. She wears jaunty '50s slacks

and a barnyard-red paisley blouse.
As she descends the stairs
with a carpe-diem stride

she angles her head toward us.
"Must sally forth," she says
"before the sun's gone!"

She seems the current age
of my daughters, yet not dark-clad
Mother at that age after

my father's death. She's the mother
from 8mm movies, walking to Chestnut Street
or cooking hot dogs at Lake Sebago.

Then she's gone
past the landing: the number forty-nine
palpable in our air.

The age my father died, when
mourning almost strangled
Mother's breath. Reo's age

and mine, when first
he touched my skin
and from inside my eyes

I began to see more
emerge from transparent air
than had appeared to me before.

Riffle riff

Here's a notion: riffle through a drawer of buttons knuckle-deep. Fingers tensed at the clatter. Riffle and recoil.

Bronze or gold bulbous, ecru as age-yellowed white. Tangerine or turquoise like '40s polka dots, tiny with rhinestone nubs. Plastic in the Notions Department.

Which buttons are as cute as they're all said to be?

Post-Depression thrift, snipped from old clothes. Buttons translucent, so dark backs gleam. Powder pink, lime-green squares with rounded corners. Stitched through rear loops, they droop like '50s button earrings.

Touch them and plummet into pleated hand-me-downs. Fabrics clean but steeped in camphor. Tough luck to get them. Button your lips!

Now clothes keep spare buttons near seams or in discrete plastic bags. No riffle to replace them. No risk of lurking pearleen. Still, my mind is buttoned up.

If buttons fasten the world, how do we hang on? Its surface swamped with mottled-beige blunt spheres, sculpted tan half-domes, huge convex navy blues, small pale mother-of-pearl.

What more can I say with a button sewn onto the tip of my tongue?

I see you

                    Darkness.
A cavern in what I'd thought
a vacant lot between high houses.
Or is this a different neighbourhood?
Street lamps, now dim pools
of light absorbed past the curb.
The other sidewalk, thick dark.
No shadow to balance me behind
or show the way forward.
I grope along the alley
for stairs or a slope toward light.
But the blackness points nowhere.

A weight in my jacket pocket.
Not a flashlight, just kalamata olives
in a ziplock bag. I pierce their skin,
suck the pulp, spit the murky pits. Olive
after olive. Ah love you. All of you.

Then light so bright I can't stand
its glare. And on a bench
beside our floodlit pool: you—
finally seated between your sons.
Both in swim trunks, one texts,
the other stares into the water's glint.
I watch your blue eyes deepen
as darkness

                    spills from your lids.

January insomniac

You're Janus with two heads. One faces the past and sleeps.
The other, facing the future, hears its twin snore.

You're all about transitions, adrift in between.
You hover in thin-skinned sleep. Can't plunge to its depth

though your eyes snap shut as if you'd sneezed.
They say a sneeze expels your soul through your nose.

Bless you. But by now you're in a devilish state.
You'd forfeit that soul to sever night and day—

snoring, you abandon all hope of the sleep
that could hurtle you through tomorrow.

Old Testament God gave Adam life through his nostrils
and life, you conclude, exits where it entered.

Attached by an intake of breath. May it be a quiet one.
It's two a.m. and the night is long.

rivers of air

(for Maija Kagis)

hooked flat, inert
Maija is a fish out of water
and still she hankers

after Latvian food:
glassy-eyed mackerel
smoked intact

on the deli shelf
where golden gills
don't process air—

I worry a whole fish
though tender
would be unwieldy

for her to handle
in hospital, also smoked
Swoyska sausage hard to grill

till she's back home—
for now I buy creamy
liver paté, and until

the deli stocks large Laima bars
I choose Laima's "Riga"
chocolates, from the city

she and I knew—
this box with a picture
of Riga's spires doubled

at sunset on the Daugava River
whose water flows inside them:
their placement brief

like the tubes of air
I see shortly
in Maija's house

where they lead to her
high sun-porch bed
feed her lungs

the room crammed
with family, doctors, friends
who don't mention

the final hospital discharge
her daughter's email
soon reveals

the mackerel's amber eye
stares at nothing
and at me

Giveaway

I—A black-and-white cameo

Whatever pressed this young girl against
this old woman must have lasted
just until the shutter snapped.
The girl already peers sideways
toward her escape.

At the right edge, a slim arm hangs
from a sleeveless dress,
blends into fence posts.
On the left, a high brick wall.

Cropped so she shifts to the centre,
the thin old woman stares
to the right, the plump-cheeked
child looks to the left.

Nameless people shut inside a tin frame
seventy years ago,
left for trash after
a neighbourhood yard sale.

II—The young woman unseen past her arm

As if I don't have enough to do.
Yet again I've bowed to family pressure
and brought the child to visit the old woman.
Long trip here and back in one day.
Tricky to keep a child's dress clean.

I might as well humour the old crow
with a snapshot. Even snip it
so she's smack in the middle.
I don't need to be there.

I'll bind her to the child
in a frame's endless oval.
Then we can wait a while
before we come see her again.

The frame's flanges will grip
its thick cardboard backing.
Why bother with names
and the date we all know.

And if this oval zero remains
on the heap after we sell her things?
Who will be left to care?

III—The old woman in her backyard

How kind of her to send me
this photograph. I'm pleased
she came with the child, though
I discerned a duty visit.

Naturally, I kept my eyes impassive
as this brown oval frame.

When we posed for the picture,
I reached to hold the child's hands.
But she turned aside. Perhaps
my bony fingers frightened her.

One of my fists—veined, I know—
cramped her taut fingers.
My other hand, badly knobbed,
under her other palm.

Still, the child should know how
to behave. It may not be my place
to say, but she's too big to fidget.

Yet at that moment, I was close enough
to feel her dimpled arms. If only during
their hurried visit, these two warmed
the yard like sunlight on phlox
near the fence.

It's lovely to have this oval brooch.
Who will inherit it after I'm gone?

IV—The young girl, now an adult

I think I was three or four then.
I squinted to the left,
so I wouldn't have to see
the old lady. Like any kid
would do.

Before the camera clicked
—cameras clicked then—
I tried to wrench
my hands away. Fingers flat,
so the old lady couldn't hold them.
But her dry fingers grasped my wrist.

Look at her old pompadour!
My 1950s hair—that silly side part
and plastic bow barrette!

Amazingly, the frame is nearly
unscathed. Flanges never lifted.
Just a gouge halfway up one side,
as if I'd tried to claw my way
out of the photo.

Now this relic in the mail.
Part of me remembers that day
too well. Another part, not well
enough. Might as well unload it
on the yard-sale table.

Maybe someone will want the frame.

VII

Email to Justine

There

In the front room I seldom use
I climbed a low ladder to reach
my white teapot

         and there was my sister, her head wedged
between the bookcase and the ceiling.
Waiting, she breathed with no sound.

Months ago I'd been told she had died:
ashes spread on the ocean
before I could see her.

         Yet in my dream her hair was as dark
as she'd always kept it. She said nothing, though I listened
for her exclamation marks.

How had I overlooked her? Head hidden
but her body in view down tiers of shelves. She rested
both feet on a shelf halfway down.

         After I found her
we stepped from ladder rungs in tandem
onto the hardwood floor. We stood

         and beheld
each other, tasted the air in my room. My sister's
lips didn't move. My own mouth opened

then closed without speech. *Happiness* too narrow
a word for me to pronounce, bounded
by too many letters. *Joy* too short, with too few.

before his death, Leo could eat only ice cream

vanilla ice cream drizzles
from the newfangled frozen treats
my grandfather Frank made to sell
at his corner store
dipping them in chocolate
inserting wooden sticks
when his brain hemorrhaged
and he died at 49
the same age my father Leo died
after 20 years married
to Frank's daughter Rose
the same number of years Frank
was married to my grandmother Yohanna

Rose loved the ice cream
Leo brought home each week
from Paret & Lamouree
neither Leo nor Rose troubled
that she became plump
though she grew lean again
after he died
when she turned sick
and moved from 77 Bly Square
to Florence's large house
where we sisters Florence, Justine
Natalie and Adele stayed close
until Rose died at 77
the same age as Justine
who died yesterday

when her brain hemorrhaged
before, she'd thought, her next day
of work, where she'd pep up
her tour group with puzzles and songs
but she lay comatose
in hospital the day before
August 23, Rose's birthday
also the day they removed
Justine's air tube
though she still breathed
until my daughter Joanna's birthday
August 25, dying at night
as Yohanna had died
not found until the next day
when she hadn't rolled down
her hat-shop awning or swept
her sidewalk, still in the job
she'd loved since before
Justine's birth on April 9, 1938

Justine who chose her mobile home
for its post box 4938
and whose favourite flavour
she always said
was vanilla fudge

Along the Ottawa River

A blue heron dips its neck
for fish. Wades in Britannia Bay
below white clouds, calm
as the current. Widens its wings

and flies away. Legs long
and slim: my sister who walked
her west coast trails. She's
in ashes, smoke, the sea.

Near the wharf, a dragonfly
clutches a monarch
butterfly. Orange
still flutters. The dragonfly pins
the black-lined wings
flat in dirt. At Island Park

a toppled poplar, thick trunk firm.
I touch bark that's furrowed
as my sister's skin.
The tree's roots severed
moist from soil. They thrust
toward sun
and clasp the sky.

sweet life

you nod off to sleep
thinking of
your sister Justine
and wake up
thinking of
a roast beef sandwich
neither of you
non-meat eaters
would have eaten

your brain healthy
you hope
though convoluted
you know
but hers—since
a blood vessel burst—
empty
of any thought

the roast beef maybe
for ruth betty
her birth name
she saw as
her baby name
yet up till the end
her spoon scraped
bowls of brown betty
she liked to call
ruth betty
its buttered brown sugar
thick on her tongue

Midnight last night

Lafayette Avenue in my hometown, Suffern.
My daughter Joanna and I just finished her birthday lunch
at Yang Ming, and she's helping me buy a hat

for my sister's memorial service. A straw hat with flowers.
Justine lived in Palm Springs, so would have liked straw,
though both Suffern stores

are shelving summer hats. Still, the first one I try
is perfect. A purple cloche, brimless, daisies
across the crown. Expensive.

A hat my grandmother Yohanna might have sold, I say
to Joanna, who checks a sale at the other store and
suggests we go there. But I found this hat fast

and it suits me. The salesman tells us
these stores are co-owned: he'll sell me
the hat I want at the other store's price—

The phone rings and I'm jerked awake, pick up
so quickly the cord unplugs. When I reconnect,
my sister Florence calls back. She says Justine's breath

stopped at midnight. While Joanna's real-world birthday
was ending. My mouth dries as if I'd swallowed
too much soy sauce at noon.

Airtime

Let me answer the question you never asked me
now that I know you asked our other sisters.

I'm afraid of heights, can't abide operetta.
So rule out the funicular and the Follies

in what you called your standard tour for guests.
Its one size wouldn't fit me. Nor did your

housewarming gift, "standard" you said again
as I thanked you. Postcards from your photo career

arranged as a plastic poster. *Night-lit skyscrapers*
in L.A. *Miss you* in Maine. *Sizing up the bull*

in New Mexico. Photos of the country
I chose to leave thirty years before

sent in welcome to the new home I'd found.
Your poster stowed in my basement, hastily hung

in my study the odd time you came here
and rummaged through my rooms.

Now your sudden death.
I've carried the postcards upstairs

where I can see them without your frame, detect
what our words hadn't said.

If only you could have understood the brick house
I live in, tall maples in my yard. If only I could have

stood your jaunts in the desert near your mobile home.
If only you had asked me why I never

came to visit you. I don't go to the country I left.
That slant answer might have cleared the air.

while my sister dies

I landed as soon as I leapt
into the Grand Canyon, Justine would have said
and grinned, to prove to her sisters
that she'd have selected this death

brain's abrupt end, threads of breath

bus-tour clients in the lobby, all set
for her to unveil the games she'd amassed
to amuse them through South Dakota:
Justine their queen

inert in a fourth-floor hotel room

we other sisters text and talk only
of her, and doctors clamp a vessel despite
the damage done: her brain flooded
and drowned before she knew

her full-tilt arms and legs won't stir

the limelight that heightened her colour
now green and sour for us sisters, who wait
to hear she's been lifted from a hospital bed
in Sioux Falls, her ashes

flown west, alone in the silent sea

Email to Justine

Lots happening! So much
to catch up on.
Talked to our sisters often—
sometimes three times a day, plus email
and Skype. Loved that! Wish you
and I had done the same.

Also in touch with cousins
I hadn't spoken to in eons.
Judy says it's more than six years.
Will Skype with Susie and Eli tomorrow.

Finally called your friend Gayle
who's still in Ottawa for the summer.
Would you believe she's just
five blocks away, and once
sang in my choir? Will meet her for tea
when things settle down.

On a different note, I now understand
sitting shiva. I know
what you'll think :-) Really, I'm still
just like you—see no need
for Jewish ritual. But our family
spent this week together.
So what if we used cyberspace?
We're two generations too far from Windau
to meet in our old family home.

Also, Ed found a great photo of you.
We've sent it around and everyone
likes it a lot. You're wearing
your red-and-white textured scarf
and look really happy!

Much more to say, and I'd love
to hear from you. Tried Skyping you
this morning, but you didn't pick up.
Maybe your Skype address changed?
My laptop told me your old address
(live:justinehill_1) isn't valid.
In any case, Skype said
you are Away.

memory

how can my brain remember
to close my lips for the *m*

lower the tip of my tongue for the *s*
touch the roof of my mouth for the *d*

so I can utter the words
my sister died

after my sister's brain forgot
how to breathe

VIII

Directions to Suffern NY circa 1950

tangled in flourishes

I

white clapboard, blue shutters
the young skin of home
tints to sepia
as each year, damp or blustery air
softens the wood
also the tan shingles nailed on later
this outer layer
exposed to days and nights
the shield
of pale inner skin
the shield
exposed to days and nights
this outer layer
also the tan shingles nailed on later
softens the wood
as each year, damp or blustery air
tints to sepia
the young skin of home
white clapboard, blue shutters

II

in all directions
my first home follows me
with pairs of glass eyes
two pairs east and west
two north and south

shutters, later outlined
and shaded
in brown and beige
like eyeliner and shadow
highlight these eyes
that see the front yard

their glass reflects
the curve of my back
as I turn away

III

a turtle stays home
unless it sticks out its neck
or lumbers into the sun

secure in the shell
joined to its spine and ribs
it's a homebody

who enlarges its home
slowly as it grows
to new dimensions

do turtles live eighty years
because they hunker down
in their homes

or because they can breed
so many more who bask
in homebound joys?

an empty turtle shell
is not a real estate ad
it's an obituary

IV

all sharp angles
her body too skinny to house her
its upper floors completed
just a few weeks ago

her perfume: wood resin
that scents flawless wallboard
she blushes a rosy tone
and her doors, flush
with their moulding, varnished
as fingernails

ample hips will later allow her
to plump in comfy
chairs, thighs will cushion her
on the couch, her bloodstream
will murmur within her

she'll drink tea in sun
that freckled her arms, wear slippers
pushed behind warped doors

inhale to enter her house
exhale, and breath
will welcome her home

V

absence
of fences

the straight line you make
from your short yard
curly with myrtle

the chasm
you cross

years that strain ahead
before they saunter
along the old street

zigzag back
to your pillared front door

VI

build your house, Mies van der Rohe
said, and showed me how
form is function, less is more

Bauhaus lines femur-long, double-use
parts like tongues that enunciate and
taste, sheet glass that lets you look within

thanks, Mies: I was too tangled in flourishes
to see what you called "skin and bones"
architecture, too overgrown to be it

78 peas

Wrinkled and limp as newborn babes, 78 peas
circumnavigate sister Willa's plate. She turns
them into a raspberry for fat Mrs. Van Dusen.

Blown like my chance to learn to blow raspberries.
Busy squishing my way outside Mother,
a newborn babe wrinkled and limp as 78 peas.

Willa watched the taxi take Mother for two weeks.
Childbirth rest before home to three kids who are
turning Mrs. Van Dusen into a fat raspberry.

With *foodie* just sister Nell's word for food,
no fresh peas for urban folk, frozen unknown,
78 peas wrinkle and limp from their tepid tin can.

Father inscribes to Mother: *Thanks to Adele.*
754 pages of Ayn Rand, who knells for any
Mrs. Van Dusens that turn into sweet raspberries.

What sum of peas might she have imposed
to get me a brother or new sister, limp babes
wrinkled as Willa, now 78 like those peas she recalls
as Mrs. Van Dusen. A red-faced raspberry.

its glitz   a glare

neon orange edges
                 flash along white walls
     blaze
       into the neighbourhood
sear sedate blocks
            of square-metred cement
      shaped
         like obese bricks with slim
     orange steel trim

once Otto's car lot
                    bought
the Ur-urge for condos
       urgent
cash   urban crash
built within code but o
range of homespun colours
      overlooked

these fiery lines will fade
from sun   and as the rain   snow
      flotsam in wind
   splatter   white expanse
tailpipes   tenant cars
        smudge fresh-paint walls
   to match black-laced snowdrifts

by the time orange edges dim
some neighbours
                          may be used to them
but from my third-floor perch
an oak screens the view
shows robins' breasts
                 russet leaves
on burnt-sienna brick

each fall I'll flinch
as orange flares
        fierce for me   as new
since no one chose
                    tan or green infill
        or *ange*   *de dieu*
how about *sacré bleu*

Road trip back

When I reach the road sign to Longueil
I've stared through the windshield
for hours. That helps me find the realm
where she inhabits the sign.
She fits inside it, green and flat,
inflates as I approach.
Swirls wisped hair
to curtain her lips, as if still a student
kissing her professor. She smirks,
to remind me he was my husband.

Years and kilometres collide.
I'm deep in New Brunswick when I see
Dorchester's sign. My old colleague
awaits me, compressed
in the sign's white letters.
He coalesces, as my fingers recall
the heft of his hair. He flexes
squashed quads and runs
to keep pace with my tires.

Even I strut from a nearby sign.
My couture shimmers.
Pale blue suits with shoulder pads
hang closeted in Moncton's sign,
crease-free till I read the place name.
In Nova Scotia I also slosh
from the narrow sign to Upper Tantallon.
Its long surface reeks of dank walls:
cottage plywood and my pregnant belly swell.

A/C floods the car as if for that humid
summer with no swims in Tantallon Bay.
Water frigid, skin numb. The shivers.
Road ghosts, mythic as Tantalus,
slow my speed through sudden curves.
They flaunt how the bay still hides tentacled
seaweed, zigzags its schools of silver fish.

late afternoon bath

along the hypotenuse
                    like a hi-fi needle
that vibrates with music

a cone of light
jiggles its idea
             of warm oiled water

a leg hopping to the beat
                    above slats
angled on the wall ahead

the side window
blinded, shrunk into stripes
                 as sun splashes

like the white light
             that will beckon us all
with just such flare

Prost!

You can't snag an invitation to this dinner party,
one of few you'd dress up to attend.
All guests, seated around the table, gone.

You sprawl near your father's 8mm projector:
its whirring heat, flecked light, musty sugar smell.
On your lap, a styrofoam box of burger and fries.

You gaze at the matriarch and patriarch. His moustache,
thick and white, defines his face. Her eyes crinkle
as she kisses him, clowns at you.

Their son gesticulates, fingers splayed
for emphasis. One daughter lifts her fork to feed
her husband cake. Son and daughters—your father

and six aunts. In rimless glasses, flowered prints.
Your father's head keeps time when their mouths enlarge
in song. Goblets clink to fifty years: 1938 on silent film.

As Aunt Leah talks to the camera, you read her lips.
Watch your hand touch Uncle Max's arm. You or
your Aunt Leah smiles into his rippled brow.

The projector hums. You raise your Coke, lock eyes
with your face at the table. The cheeks curl upward.
You hear yourself laugh.

Directions to Suffern NY circa 1950

1   Ride your Trek 10-speed bicycle
up Wayne Avenue and turn
into the driveway at what was once #145.
Continue along the gravel
on the tricycle your sister outgrew.

Look straight ahead as your sister
hops onto the foot-bar
and tickles your neck
before she leaps off.
Part your lips in laughter
on your journey
toward the garage.

Your father screwed wood blocks
to the pedals
so your saddle shoes
can propel you forward.
Your mother won't bother you
to slather sunscreen
on the pink skin
around your sunsuit straps.

Park your trike beside the maple
next to the driveway.
Ring your bell five times
and demand a fill-up.
Your sister will stuff
your conical seat springs
with gravel gas.

2   Wait for summer, then activate
your Keystone air conditioner
in your attic bedroom in Ottawa.
Go back downstairs for an hour.

Open the attic door off the bedroom
you share with your sister.
Squeeze past the algebra book
and crinoline
one of you left on the dresser
and ascend the stairway.

The odour of dry heat
on dark wood leads
to a stencilled pink crib
and picture of Gram with black hair.

For once, don't be so obedient:
touch the pine lamps and tables
from the brown bungalow
your family lived in
those years before you were born.
Which nick on the table
marks the time your father dropped
the bronze bowl full of almonds?

Climb once more to your attic
with its 46-inch flat screen.
Though that bedroom will be cool by now
you're where you want to be
when your parched nostrils constrict.

3   If the operator picks up
your cell phone signal, call Suffern 605
and ask for Mrs. W.G. Wenman.
Praise her house on the postcard
of Wenman Villa. Though her *Rooms
and Garages* at 145 Wayne Avenue
pre-date 1950, their interior
displays the house your parents bought
months before your birth.

Blink through your umbilical cord
and glimpse the world
of your young parents, who by middle age
were not around for you to know.

Reserve one of Mrs. Wenman's *Modern
and Distinctive Tourist Accommodations*
with a *Private and Connecting Bath.*
In winter, check that *Steam Heat* works.

Should you choose the first room
upstairs, pull the closet's glass knob
to hang your full-length clothes.
And fall into that homey
bed near the door.

Mrs. Wenman will be pleased
you found her card
but best not to mention an internet.

4   Focus on your job in Ottawa.
Give birth to a daughter, raise her
and take her to Suffern circa 2000.
When a teenager answers the door
at 145 Wayne Avenue
introduce yourselves. He prefers
his Game Boy and will let you
wander the house alone.

Rummage around. Regard each room
as your daughter might view it.
Encourage her questions.

Show her the second door to the porch.
Yes, breezes did reach you at dinner
on scorcher days like these.
Smell the acetic acid
in the rear corner of the cellar.
Other fathers didn't build
their own darkrooms.
She's right, the house does feel
less spacious than the home
you've always described.

Leave quickly, with thanks, when the boy's
father arrives and ushers you
from the upstairs hall.
Once back in Canada, mail a note.
They won't respond, but offer
to purchase the yellow wall-lamp
your mother bought for the den.

5   Lift the hardboard lid
        of the five-inch eyeglass case.
        Easy, since it has no spring
        but beware the small nails
        at the bottom corners.
        Stroke the blue felt lining, rubbed thin.
        LEO HIRSHMAN, OPTOMETRIST
        embossed in gold.
        Observe your father's penmanship
        on the label he pasted
        inside the lid: *Jan. 13, 1951.*

        When he comes home from his office
        and presents you with the case
        ease your pink pearleen glasses
        onto the bridge of your nose.
        Curl the side arms to the base of your ears.

        Though you need glasses only
        for reading, request
        your parents' permission
        to wear them at dinner that night.
        From your place at the table
        beam as your father looks at you.
        Savour your parents' comments
        about how your frames fit your face.

        The next day, Miss Ponds will announce
        your brand-new glasses
        to the Grade 1 class.
        Cringe for six decades.

6   Click on the link your cousin emails you.
Pore over photos of familiar rooms
furnished to help sell
this Wayne Avenue property.

Resolve to write science fiction
when you grow up. Straightaway, start
chapter one: "Four hundred miles
from Suffern, each room
of the 1950s house appears
on a screen in Ottawa.
The rooms are as they will be
seventy years in the future."

Photoshop the aluminum shelves
out of the master bedroom.
Can you edit the grey Ikea chairs
so they sag like the black ones
in your parents' room?
Sit with your parents.
Refuse to go to bed
until they explain
the space-time continuum
in a way you understand—

why continuous blue lines
your father painted on basement poles
remain and he doesn't.

7   Friday night, turn on your iPhone.
         When you key in your password
         your father will answer his office phone.
         Sabbath candles are lit in the kitchen
         so wish him *Good Shabbos*.

         If it's not Friday night
         grab your Evian water and walk downtown
         to 61 Lafayette Avenue:
         Family Vision Care
         Ira Clement O.D.
         Don't get sidetracked by altered
         buildings. You'll know
         the brick storefront
         with its optometry office
         your father established.

         Or call: you also know the number
         still printed on the door.
         If no one answers
         peek through the plate glass.
         That picture of the peddler
         selling eyeglasses to the farm family.
         Who painted it?
         Try to recall what your father said
         when he hung it upstairs in the hall.

8   No point in squinting at street numbers
         to find your house
         at 145 Wayne Avenue.
         A left pillar numbered 151
         and a right one 153
         flank your front door.

         Think of the Cold War in 1950:
         the five-foot gong
         hung suddenly in your ballfield
         for fathers to ring
         when the Commies attacked.

         Then consider the mayhem
         as the century flipped and slid
         into 9/11. Emergency vehicles
         now on alert to locate
         double lots like yours
         24/7 when the terrorists strike.

         Begin, if you can, to visualize
         the house: two numbers
         for one family whose left side
         splits from its right.
         Enter your central front hall
         and allow your eyes to adjust.

Stare to the left
as 145 changes to 151
near your dining room table
long with aunts and uncles
plus cousins close to your age.
A parent at each end.

Steady yourself and peer to your right.
Notice how 145 becomes 153
at the bottom
of the narrow stairs
your mother summoned you down
to hand you
Suffern's newspaper
the week of your father's obituary.

9   Sing "O Canada" until you're hoarse.
Press weights until your biceps ache
as if you'd lifted a thick cotton
American flag on its solid-wood pole
and lugged it down the driveway.
Slant it into the iron tube
your father installed in the soil.

You can place your palm on your heart
and sing "The Star Spangled Banner"
but don't expect the flag to fly.

Ignore your house with its blue shutters.
It will always be there.

Remember: you're the one
who packed your plaid suitcase
and flew from Suffern
to that big midwest town
where Wolfe and Proust grew
in quadrangle grass, and
friends, like-minded as ivy on brick
classroom walls, clustered around you.

Later, accompany one friend
in an urban direction.
Insert geography behind you:
cross countries and decades.
Settle, but when sunlight illuminates
grey hairs, pluck Proust
or Wolfe off your shelf.

Trample the borders you once
constructed. Sponge their dust
from your skin and ramble
in the shade
of Suffern's tree-lined days.

10 A bus ticket from New York NY
to Suffern NY may not get you there
even if you've travelled
that ShortLine route
untold times before.
Agent 24 may joke that you seem
too young for the senior fare
but she'll take your $11.75
in exchange for what looks like a ticket.

Wear your glasses.
Still, you'll be left clutching
a slip of white paper.
Read the three words across the top
printed in large bold caps:
NOT FOR PASSAGE

Notes ⌒⌒

"Ebreju kapi" is for Natalie Ventura, my sister, who translated Levin Hirschmann's diary from old German to modern German, and then to a fascinating English book.

"He leads me in Yiddish, which I don't speak" is in memory of Moses Finkman in Ventspils.

"Karfi"—Mount Karfi is still home to birds of prey. But no one knows what became of the last Minoans. They were forced up Mount Karfi and never seen again. When I sat on that peak, I sensed their human presence amid their stone ruins. What had heartened these people to survive for hundreds of years away from the sea and the land they loved?

"when the longing overtakes her" is for Carolyn Molson, who comes from Little Bay Islands and welcomes everyone who travels there.

"charged landscape" describes the wind farm in Chateaugay, New York, where wind turbines cover the hills in all directions.

"brother Karl duck?" uses two Marx Brothers movies: *Duck Soup* and *The Cocoanuts*. It's in *The Cocoanuts* that Mr. Hammer (the hotel owner) says to Chico, "Now, here is a little peninsula, and, eh, here is a viaduct leading over to the mainland." And Chico replies, "Why a duck?" Later, Mr. Hammer interrupts Chico: "It's … It's deep water, that's why a duck. It's deep water."

"Crescent" is for Erica Martin, my daughter.

"Angled" is for Wanda Procyshyn, who lent me this water-colour one summer. It's painted by her relative, a former cartoonist for *The Halifax Chronicle*.

"15 fragments" is for Lonni Sue Johnson.

All poems in the section "Email to Justine" are in memory of Justine Hill, my sister, who died on August 25, 2015. Her birth name was Ruth Betty Hirshman.

"Midnight last night" is for Joanna Martin, my daughter.

"78 peas" is for Florence Baturin, my sister. The names Willa and Nell are a nod to the poem's form: a villanelle.

Acknowledgements ⌣

Thanks to the editors of the following journals, where earlier versions of some poems in this book first appeared.

The Antigonish Review: "Airtime," "Assupen," "*Ebreju kapi,*" "Jigged marbles," "Lost thread," "Onward," "She would recognize a sonnet"

Canadian Authors Association *Byline*: "fog"

Contemporary Verse2 (CV2): "78 peas," "imaginary Greek etymology"

The Dalhousie Review: "26 Pils Street," "Giveaway," "January insomniac," "Moonscape," "There"

EVENT: "15 fragments," "I hear the comb caress her hair"

The Fiddlehead: "Armour," "Heidi costume doll talks of her sixty years as my prize in a childhood writing contest"

ottawater: "Angled," "Bathwater reverie," "early backstage," "I see you," "inflected echoes," "late afternoon bath," "sweet life"

Parchment: "after the fact," "*Hepatica*"

Poemeleon: "Riffle riff"

Qwerty: "Billy," "Latvian turf"

Tree Reading Series chapbook winner: "Directions to Suffern NY circa 1950"

Vallum: "memory"

White Wall Review: "a sign," "brother Karl duck?," "buckled into the sky," "charged landscape," "summed up sonnet," "These things happen in the news"

Thanks again to Natalie Ventura, whose poetry showed me the way.

Thanks also to my stalwart critique group: long-term members Marie-Andrée Auclair, Steve de Paul and Rona Shaffran, and our mentors Nadine McInnis, David O'Meara and Deanna Young. And thanks to Stuart Ross for his advice and guidance.

Mostly, my thanks to Michael Mirolla for his belief in this book and for publishing Canadian poets in his Essential Poets Series.

About the Author ∿

Adele Graf grew up outside New York City and immigrated to Canada in 1968. She has worked as a writer and editor, and taught writing in the public and private sectors in Halifax and Ottawa. She lives in Ottawa with her spouse. Her first book of poetry, *math for couples*, was published by Guernica Editions in 2017 and shortlisted for the Archibald Lampman Award. Her first chapbook, *a Baltic Friday early in grey*, was published later that year by above/ ground press. A second chapbook, *Directions to Suffern NY circa 1950*, won the Tree Reading Series chapbook prize and was published by Tree in 2018.

Printed in February 2021
by Gauvin Press,
Gatineau, Québec